Best Practices In Organizational Development

A Systems Approach to Achieving Business Potential

Quin Childress

Copyright © 2014 by Quin Childress

All rights reserved.

ISBN-13: 978-1503116672
ISBN-10: 1503116670

DEDICATION

To my wife Pat, a fantastic lady, terrific life partner, and my best friend. Without her encouragement this book could never have been written.

Contents

	Introduction	1
1	What is Organizational Development?	3
2	Best Practices for Leadership Effectiveness	13
3	Organizational Framework and Management System Components	21
4	Process for Organizational Development	37
5	Road Map for Organizational Development	43
6	Tool Kit for Organizational Development	47

Introduction

There is already an overwhelming amount of information on how to manage and develop organizations. So, why is another approach to the subject needed? From our direct experience in management consulting, we know that leaders struggle with adapting their organizations to keep up with change. We believe a better methodology is needed to generate positive change and get results faster. While there are many good solutions, they are often presented as fragmented pieces that can be confusing to those who may not understand that each piece is in fact part of an interactive system.

We felt that globally accepted best practices for Organization Development (OD) needed to be fully defined and presented in a more simplified, straightforward approach. Through our hands-on experience working with management and employees in many different environments, we've developed an effective change management process for organizational development. Using our system, measurable results in productivity will typically be evident in the first 90 days. If top management commits to a 12 month process, full implementation of best practices can be achieved in the first year. Beyond 12 months, a sustaining plan holds the gains achieved and maintains a continuously improving management system.

The approach presented in our methodology will show how to create an effective performance management system that works in a wide variety of sectors. Since all organizations have the common elements of employees, customers, work processes, and business strategy, we've developed a process for building a customized organizational structure around these elements. Combined with a sustainable system of continuous improvement, the process enables management to get ahead of external forces and to stay ahead. We know by experience that the process works as described and is user-friendly to implement if the prescribed routines are followed. We've had examples of front line supervisors who, after reading the material (with no training from us), implemented the process, and got positive results in just a few weeks.

The content presented in this book is a strategy that shows what is needed to make organizational development work in your organization. While some activities are shared that show how the process is carried out, readers should not expect to see within this book all the activities needed for full implementation. Although the steps are the same for each organization, a designated facilitator is recommended to coordinate specific activities, tools, etc. that are applicable for the needs of each. Organizations must be careful not to blindly adopt new philosophies like organizational development. Decide if/how you can use these methods to make adjustments that satisfy the distinctive needs of your organization.

CHAPTER 1

What is Organizational Development?

There are many definitions. Our definition of organizational development takes into consideration the characteristics commonly accepted and used by organizations with proven success.

Definition

Organizational development is a system-wide process of planned change, managed from the top and aimed at improving overall organizational effectiveness. The process objective is to create a synchronized system with the purpose of maximizing value creation for a specifically defined customer. Ultimately, organizational development is designed to sustain the organization over the long term.

Organizational development is a coordinated process used to make corrections in beliefs, values, attitudes and organizational structures so they can better adapt to changing technology, external forces and business challenges. Changes are accomplished through the components of mission, values, strategy, leadership, culture, information, rewards, work policies and procedures. Organizational development creates new methods to maintain organizational health now and into the future.

Several Themes

With all of our materials, methods and tools, we repeat several themes that are necessary to make organizational development work. They are prioritized in order of importance as follows:

- Leadership
- Culture
- Execution
- Accountability

These themes must be fully developed across the organization so that they are observably important, practiced up and down the chain of command and across all departmental boundaries. For an organization to be healthy, these themes must be blended into a forward moving system. The system has to be aimed at a common goal and must constantly improve effectiveness toward accomplishing that goal.

Because of constant change, traditional structures and control systems that rely on hierarchy, rules and policies inhibit an organization's ability to focus on a common objective and respond to change rapidly. The components and process laid out in our methodology describe a process for rapid development and alignment that blend these necessary themes into one focused, high performing management system.

Four Basic Elements Determine an Organization's Performance

We usually think of organizations as single entities. However, in reality they are collections of people who usually act in their own self-interest. To achieve high performance, the actions of people within an organization must be aligned and synchronized with one another, and with the strategic goals of the organization.

Because individual behaviors determine an organization's success over time, it is necessary to first establish a baseline to understand how the character of an organization (i.e., the culture) influences each individual's behavior and actions that affects his or her performance. The ability for individuals to perform is determined by four elements present in every organization. How these elements are managed determines the organization's behavior, its distinctive character, how it looks to the internal and external world, and how well people perform. These four elements are:

1. **Structure.** What is the organizational hierarchy? What are the lines of authority and responsibilities in the organization? How many layers are in the hierarchy, and how many people does each layer have?

2. **Decision-making.** Who decides what? How many people, and what levels, are required to make a decision? Where does one person's decision-making authority end and someone else's begin? Is decision-making allowed at the most informed level?

3. **Motivators.** What goals, incentives, and career choices do people have? How are they rewarded? What are they encouraged to prioritize and care about in their work?

4. **Communication.** How is knowledge and information shared and communicated? How are cross-functional activities coordinated? How are expectations, accountability and progress communicated? How is performance measured? How is information transferred from the people who have it to the people who need it?

For organizational development to produce results, clear instructions, expectations, and practices for each element must be spelled out in order for the organization to function effectively. How these elements are defined *and managed* determines overall organizational performance.

Goals of Organizational Development

Organizational development concentrates a system-wide effort to change individual behavior so that the focused activity of individuals is disciplined, and aimed directly at achieving specific common objectives.

Many organizations have successfully completed organization development initiatives. As a model for OD success, their efforts typically consist of defining and sustaining management competencies in the following areas:

- Vision, Values and Mission
- Authority and Control

- Strategic Thinking, Planning, and Execution
- Program Development and Implementation
- Evaluation, Learning and Accountability
- Human Resource Management
- Organizational Culture
- Management Systems and Structures
- Legal Compliance, Fiscal Management and Public Accountability
- Resource Development
- Stakeholder Relationships
- Collaboration

In the approach we prescribe, definition and implementation of these competencies are applied based on the unique traits/needs of the organization, rather than cloning or adopting from academic theory or another organization's model.

Our Solution

A best practices method is available that can be adapted to any organization. It is accomplished by following the simple straight-forward approach presented in the following chapters. This disciplined logical process creates a new management system with these dynamic attributes:

- Performance is driven in a culture where people are focused on positive, forward change, and encouraged to innovate
- Effective managers emphasize values and operational sophistication, and rules and hierarchy are de-emphasized
- Leadership is distributed by sharing authority, information knowledge and data throughout the organization
- Employees are utilized effectively with focus less on activity and more on results connected to the mission
- Sustained excellence appears when all the key elements are connected to each other and simultaneously aligned to the marketplace

When and Why Should Organizational Development be Used?

First, leadership must recognize the need for change.

Many organizations and management teams fail to see the need for organizational development. They unwittingly neglect the needs of the organization or business system in favor of reactionary steps that are taken without considering internal and external facts and forces that should be new priorities for change and development.

Ongoing and systematic examination of the business environment will provide the rationale and direction for organizational development efforts. As a starting point, we recommend using an assessment process to effectively filter priorities to ensure the most strategic benefit. The assessment defines why change is necessary and provides direction for prioritizing change efforts.

Most change initiatives have a low percentage of success. Too often, management embarks upon a change program without fully understanding the costs in time, energy, money, and effort. The result is usually less than successful, and may alienate the very people who need to help make it work. For organizational development to succeed, management must lead the initiative and follow a well-defined, and openly communicated path to improvement.

Bottom-line, our experience with OD shows it only fails when there is a lack of leadership from the top. Usually, this is exhibited by failure in organizational alignment, synchronized action, and accountability.

Key Areas of Change in Organizational Development

While organizational development is a beneficial effort, the process often generates tension among participants. This is to be expected. Even without internal change, external pressures to stay ahead of the curve always generate some level of anxiety that must be managed. When moving an organization from old practices to alignment with accepted best practices, a level of discomfort is normal. While this "creative tension" is a positive dynamic, it must be understood and managed in order for healthy development to happen.

Our history with change management shows high performers in the organization move toward the desired change more quickly than everyone else. Many organizations make the mistake of getting hung up on moving lower performers to a higher level. Instead, management must work more with the middle performers to move them to the new and higher level. By doing this, the bulk of the people are moved to a higher level sooner and toxic tension is reduced. If the change methods are intuitive and make sense, middle performers are more likely to understand the change, appreciate the development, and are more willing to be coached through the process. Taking this approach achieves critical mass faster, accelerates focus and progress, and reduces time to accomplish objectives.

Create the Framework for Cultural Change

Most efforts at cultural change fail because they are not linked to improving the organization's production outcomes. Cultural change gets real when your aim is to create value-added output. If you want to change the culture, you must first ask, "change from what to what?" An evaluation of the current work environment is needed to assess the organization's need and ability to change. Obvious questions are: "Where does change need to begin? What are the change objectives? How do we do it?"

A disciplined method for the desired change must be defined and followed. Our organizational development methodology is based on research studies of why change efforts succeed or fail and identifies steps needed to start and carry out positive change. To be successful, change management must deliberately address two dimensions of change: the business dimension, and the people dimension.

Business Dimension of Change

The business dimension of change includes several common elements. These are the standard elements of a business change effort that managers feel most comfortable managing and include the following actions:

- Identifying business needs or opportunities
- Defining project scope, objectives and action plans
- Designing business solutions around new processes, work procedures, systems and organizational structure
- Implementing solutions into the organization

People Dimension of Change

Research shows that problems with the people dimension of change are the most commonly cited reason for failures. In our experience, helping managers be effective sponsors and coaches for cultural and individual change is the most critical success factor overall.

People development and cultural change mechanics must result in a dynamic culture focused on the individual and team performance needed to meet organizational objectives. To succeed, people from top to bottom need a system of cultural and personal development. For positive change to happen, people development will include these actions:

- Developing leadership and management ahead of staff development
- Recruiting, hiring, and retaining the best people, putting the right people in the right places, and moving the wrong ones out, or re-positioning for the right fit
- Defining performance management in a routine discipline of setting goals, following through with action, and holding people accountable
- Installing learning systems that identify key areas to concentrate training and development
- Focusing on coaching and mentoring as a key component of leadership development

Link Rewards to Performance

To change behavior, rewards must be linked to performance and the connection must be crystal clear. A performance culture recognizes, appreciates and respects individual and team contribution and rewards it. If people know what's valued and recognized, they will concentrate their work to be more successful. Performers must get rewarded more than the non-performers.

Deal With Negative Performance and Behavior

If there are no negative consequences for poor performance, then people see accountability as a sham. When there are no consequences for negative behavior, a few non-performers impede performance of co-workers to the extent that an entire organization can be sub-optimized.

Develop Mechanisms for Building a Healthy Work Environment

Every organization has an internal social environment that leans either positive or negative. Senior management is responsible for leading the effort to create a positive work experience for all employees. Management's words and actions translate into the ability or inability to create a positive performance culture. If management is historically rooted in a culture of corporate hierarchy, command-and-control methods, and/or reactionary management, and appears be inconsistent in implementing the cultural change needed, then employees interpret management to be resistant to change.

Division within an organization can also develop between work units. Structure divides an organization into units designed to perform certain jobs. By focusing on the objectives unique to each functional unit, it is easy for them to disconnect from a common purpose, create silos, and potentially generate conflict across the organization by pitting departments against each other. A key component to breaking down departmental silos is to develop methods to collectively discuss, challenge, and solve issues caused by internal separation.

The process for organizational development presented in Chapter 4 is designed to begin and work through all the action required to build a healthy high-performing work environment.

The Importance of Open Dialogue

You cannot have a healthy work environment and high performing culture without open dialogue. Open dialogue starts when people go in with unrestricted minds. When they're not limited by distorted perceptions or private agendas they are open to new information.

To make open dialogue a reality there must be a high level of safety to communicate openly. People need to know that their ideas won't be ignored or shot down. Safety in communications must be part of the organization's value system.

When people speak openly and candidly, they express their real opinions, not just those that please the power players. Because formal conversations and presentations leave little room for argument, encourage informal input and discussion. Informal dialogue is open. It encourages questions, spontaneity and analytical thinking. Informality makes it easier to get to the truth.

Open communication improves the dynamics of a group by expanding the group's capacity to get to real issues and solve bigger problems. It can be energizing and create self-confidence, optimism and unity. Robust open dialogue brings out reality, even when it makes people uncomfortable, because it has deeper purpose and personal meaning.

Finally, open dialogue should end with closure and accountability. At the end of a meeting or discussion, people need to agree on what each person has to do and when.

From Mechanics to Dynamics

The process outlined in subsequent chapters shows how our methodology addresses all the components needed to successfully initiate and create an intuitive, dynamic organization where everyone has high expectations of results. It engages all people and work units in an effective change effort that results in positive change in work units and across the organization.

Lessons Learned

From our experience with long-term organizational development efforts, we share the following lessons with those who are considering or are engaged in organizational development work:

- Development is necessary in every organization; it can be unpleasant, and tends to be chaotic at times
- Due to many moving parts, the mechanics of organizational development can quickly become complex and overwhelming
- Development is a never-ending process
- Balancing organizational development activities and day-to-day work can be very challenging for employees and managers
- People need support to sustain the change effort
- The senior executive's role is vital for success; management team and staff direct involvement is crucial
- Consultants can hold vital roles, but they are no substitute for management and staff engagement
- Development activities must be paced to get results quickly, while allowing time for learning and resistance management
- To be successful, the process must comprehend the complexity of a business but not be overly complicated to implement.

CHAPTER 2

Best Practices for Leadership Effectiveness

Organizational Development Starts with Leadership

If the commitment is made to develop leadership first, the development process defined for the organization occurs more fluidly. In the beginning, the top leader must establish the expectation that all managers make their personal development a priority and stay ahead of the OD process.

OD will go nowhere without leadership. If effective leadership is a serious goal, and visibly practiced by management, the rest of OD becomes a systematic discipline of alignment, synchronized action, and accountability. Effective leadership eliminates much of the resistance and complexity inherent to implementation.

Best practices in leadership tend to be over-discussed and underused. Organizations with leaders who behave inconsistently make it impossible to gain alignment toward common goals. So what should be done to change leadership behaviors? The answer is to develop leadership best practices that drive consistent and predictable behavior from the organization's leaders.

The first step is to formulate leadership best practices for your organization. Best practices should be defined and developed in soft skills behavior, technical skills, administrative skills, and coaching skills. Make best practices a priority for all managers throughout the organization.

Best Practices Criteria for Senior Executives/Managers

The following behavior and performance expectations are what we've determined to be effective leadership standards. These standards should form the model and priorities for every manager throughout the organization. Using this model for every manager is essential for positive change to happen in a reasonably short time frame.

Manager Expectations of Senior Executive

As part of each manager's leadership development process, they should be given the opportunity to share their expectations of the senior executive, management team superiors and peers. These are negotiated at the beginning of the OD process and may be renegotiated as needed throughout the year. Make an "agreed upon" list with each manager. Some areas might be:

- Budget
- Personnel
- Tools
- Personal Development
- Support from Top Management and other Departments

Manager-Specific Performance Expectations

Each manager is given a job description with a list of specific expectations, goals and/or objectives that apply only to them. Some might include:

1. Personal learning and development in the areas of administrative, technical and interpersonal skills
2. Coaching and development of subordinates (who and what), succession planning for their group, or career development in another unit that would benefit the organization
3. Objectives for their Work Group development
4. Customer service improvement
5. Personal results and Work Group performance

Department-Specific Performance Expectations

Each manager contributes measurably to the bottom line in ways specific to his/her department's role in the company. Performance Plans will state what is expected in specific "value-added output" from the manager and their department(s).

General Performance Expectations

Each manager contributes to the vision, mission, and organization goals by managing themselves and their department(s) in compliance with expectations as follows:

1. The manager ensures all performance is balanced between cost and adding value
   a. Contributes to the building and growth of a high performing organization
   b. Maximizes personal contribution by contributing to the growth and success of other team members
   c. Maximizes contribution to the bottom line as defined in the organization's strategy
2. Manager's department organizational structure is functionally simple, and kept that way
   a. Builds effective structure and Organization Chart
   b. Maintains focused job descriptions
3. Department's staffing is kept at optimum levels by having the best people doing the right things, and lesser contributors moved out
   a. Has correct number of people for workload demands
   b. Has correct job assignments (people matched to job)
   c. Distributes workload fairly among employees
   d. Manages employee performance and behavior
   e. Plans and executes needed training and cross-training
4. Department's budget control is maintained
   a. Has effective cost control measures in place
   b. Leads waste reduction efforts
   c. Has a "value-added" budget mentality (economic value created with all costs and activities)

BEST PRACTICES IN ORGANIZATIONAL DEVELOPMENT

5. Department's operating policies, procedures and processes are documented in flow chart and SOP forms, and are efficient and effective
    a. Keeps process flow chart(s) up to date
    b. Keeps "Standardized Work" Operating Procedures documented and up to date
    c. Emphasizes quality and workmanship in all processes and procedures
    d. Puts discipline in place to follow procedures
    e. Streamlining efforts are ongoing (to the point of diminishing returns)
    f. Uses current techniques and technology effectively
6. Performance management plans are in place for every employee by the first month of each fiscal or calendar year, and every employee is evaluated at least every six months
    a. Employee performance plans are linked to Department strategy
    b. Department Strategy is linked to Organizational Strategic Plan
    c. Employee and Department Plans have at least one "Stretch Objective"
7. Succession planning is ongoing
    a. Key positions are identified
    b. Successors are identified and developed
    c. Career planning is included in employee Performance Plans
    d. A person is identified to step into "Acting" role for Department Manager when necessary
8. A genuine commitment to being employee, customer and supplier friendly is maintained and recognized by others
    a. Department employees demonstrate the same commitment or are held accountable
    b. Provide training as needed for consistency in work groups
9. Opportunities to improve the department are sought, and those opportunities that work are seized upon and instituted
    a. Employees are regularly (as a matter of routine) asked for input and improvement ideas
    b. Recognition is given to those who provide ideas and help implement improvements

10. A clarity of focus on organizational mission and strategic plan is maintained
    a. Department has a written strategy that demonstrates support of Organizational Plan
    b. The strategy includes a plan of execution
    c. The department strategy is developed with the involvement of Department employees
    d. Manager holds entire Department accountable for achieving planned goals and objectives through their Performance Management Plans
    e. Manager holds regular "results-oriented" meetings with employees to review progress (examples are weekly staff meetings, one-on-one coaching, performance reviews, etc.)
11. A primary commitment to the organization's success is maintained, with the manager's *own* personal success being secondary
    a. Manager seeks out "big picture" direction at all times; all decisions are first weighed against organizational needs
    b. Manager's personal success is determined by meeting expectations and competencies as defined in job description and Performance Management Plan. Organization's commitment to a win-win relationship with managers is based on "mutually agreed-upon" expectations of each other
    c. Manager takes responsibility for employees' commitment to company success
12. Responsibility is taken by the manager for his/her mistakes and errors, and they are corrected
    a. Takes ownership of Departmental results and behaviors
    b. Takes ownership of subordinate mistakes/errors and takes corrective action
13. Credit is given liberally and often to those in their department, and/or other departments who perform well
    a. Manager uses formal and informal methods to recognize employees and co-workers
    b. Rewards to employees reflect individual performance and contribution to team output
14. Unexpected problems, challenges or changes in routines are handled graciously and professionally

a. Handles self well under pressure
   b. Ensures subordinate behavior is professional with timely coaching and corrective action
15. Problems and issues are raised in a constructive manner
    a. Helps to build unity and cohesion in Management Team
    b. Regular and active contributor to Management Team development
    c. Promotes teamwork among peers and across the organization
    d. Speaks with candor while being thoughtful of other opinions
16. Problems and issues raised by others are taken constructively
    a. Open to feedback
    b. Expected to act on feedback

Meeting Expectations Determines Personal Growth in the Company, Promotions, Salary, Bonuses, etc.

Performance evaluations are given to each manager at least twice a year. During the evaluation, the manager is given the opportunity to openly provide feedback on the Senior Executive's and Management Team's performance and make refinements to expectations.

We recommend a 360 degree evaluation be completed once a year on each manager. The 360 is used to determine strengths and weaknesses, and areas for improvement. As a result of the 360 Evaluation, a Leadership Development Action Plan is completed on each manager.

A disciplined process for leadership development is vital to achieving consistent results and building/maintaining employee confidence in leadership.

Action Plan for Developing Leadership

Prior to beginning the OD process, we recommend that some level of leadership assessment and development begin ahead of the organization-wide effort. First review the following list of leadership activities and facilitate a workshop that begins the leadership development process. Steps to consider include:

1. Diagnose what is currently done to develop leadership.

2. Document findings.
3. Assess skills lacking and changes needed (generally for all managers and the management team, and specifically for each manager).
4. Create best practices manual, start small, prioritize and increase sophistication over time.
5. Get training in place for leaders.
6. Establish a firm plan of corrective action for those who lack the will or the skill.
7. Identify and communicate the reason for the changes.
8. Hold managers formally accountable for practice and results.
9. Validate steps in the system, measure results every 90 days.
10. Recognize those doing well.
11. Standardize work/standardize steps for leadership development and meeting expectations.
12. Keep searching for improvements.
13. Set high standards for behavior and performance.
14. Get rid of and heal we/they divisiveness and unite through healthy emotional behavior and open communications.

For the leadership development process to succeed, leaders need to:

- Understand leadership role and own their piece of it.
- Be a champion of positive change.
- Be present, keep people connected, help with understanding the big picture.
- Participate in and help energize the management system.
- Be accountable for staying focused on the mission.
- Drive action.
- Align and synchronize efforts across the organization.
- Create opportunities for growth and reward the right people.
- Drive out fear.
- Distribute leadership and engage leaders throughout the organization at all levels.
- Delegate responsibility through empowerment.
- Demonstrate fair and predictable behavior.

- Put the right people in the right places, recruit high. performers, develop middle performers, and move low performers up or out.
- Have positive visibility in the external environment.
- Show commitment to being on board with a team effort, excellence and winning performance with plans, action and accountability.
- Have robust staff communication (provide information and solicit input).
- Connect people across the organization, put others first.
- Develop interpersonal and people skills.
- Lead/participate in effective meetings, do not waste time in useless meetings.
- Manage all resources to get the work done.
- Select and develop talent (coaching and supervising, performance management).
- Use critical thinking and problem-solving.
- Understand the external environment.

To get all leaders/managers on board, develop a leadership toolkit that covers the basics through advanced leadership and management job requirements. Create a leadership development plan, train for specific outcomes for individuals, work groups, management team, and senior executives. Customize leadership development for the organization's immediate and long term needs. Do not train just for the sake of training. Have a plan for how managers will practice new skills and be held accountable for expectations.

Leaders Create the Behavioral Culture that They Exhibit and Tolerate

The role of leadership cannot be overemphasized in the context of organizational development. The culture of a company is dictated by the behavior of its leaders. Cultural change happens when leadership behavior changes. You measure the change in culture by measuring the change in the personal behavior of its leaders and their effect on performance and ethics of the entire organization.

CHAPTER 3

Organizational Framework and Management System Components

The Business Performance Revolution

Business models, frameworks, and methodologies – such as the Balanced Scorecard, Toyota Production System, Malcolm Baldrige Performance Excellence, and Continuous Quality Improvement – have each generated vast interest, effort and activity, and are widely used, but haven't always generated success. Each framework claims to be unique and comprehensive. Yet each offers a different perspective on performance. On the surface, the number of methods can be conflicting and confusing. How can multiple, and seemingly inconsistent, business performance frameworks and measurement methodologies exist?

They all add value. They all provide unique perspectives on performance. They all furnish managers different approaches which can assess organizational performance and provide a methodology for improvement. The key is to recognize that, despite the claims of some of the proponents of these various frameworks and methodologies, there is no one best way to view business performance. Business performance is defined differently for every organization.

Nevertheless, when we talk with academics, industrialists, non-profit and government organizations alike, there seems to be a 'pent-up demand' for a multi-faceted, yet highly adaptable, new framework – a framework which will address the needs for business performance measurement within the new competitive environment of the 21st Century. How can that demand be satisfied?

A Refined Performance Model

For years we used the Balanced Scorecard[1] for our model because it provided the greatest flexibility. The Balanced Scorecard is still widely used and very effective. Recently we've adopted a different model that is similar to the Balanced Scorecard, but more focused on a strategic approach that generates improvements in multiple outputs (including financial results).

Our revised model comes from a management system framework developed by Dr. George Labovitz, founder and CEO of Organizational Dynamics, Inc[2]. This framework is highly flexible across a diverse range of organizations and captures all the current best practices in organizational models. The ODI framework is presented in the books *The Power of Alignment* (1997), and *Rapid Realignment* (2012). The ODI framework has four competencies with leadership and culture at its core.

ODI ALIGNMENT FRAMEWORK

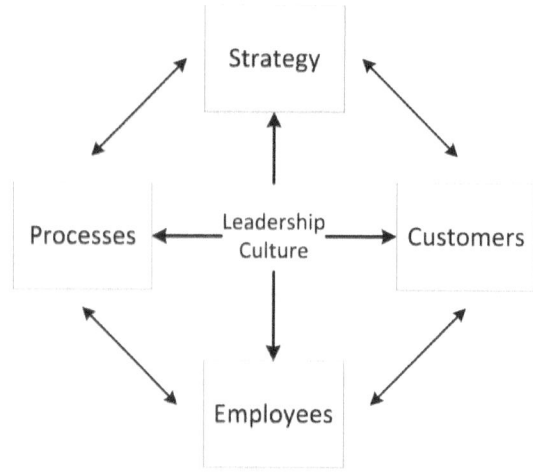

---

[1] Robert S. Kaplan, David P Norton, The Balanced Scorecard, Harvard Business School Press, 1996
[2] George Labovitz, Victor Rosansky, Rapid Realignment. McGraw Hill, 2012

For our purposes, we have made adjustments to the ODI model in the areas of customer relations, lean management principles, human development, and performance management that give us greater flexibility, accuracy, and speed when driving major change in an organization.

Employees and Work Culture

What Your Most Productive Workers Want and Need

A study conducted by The Gallup Organization[3] revealed that workers worldwide, regardless of nationality or culture, essentially wanted the same things from the work environment. The following twelve components are desired by the most productive workers (they're summarized below in order of importance, with insight from our experiences working with and interviewing thousands of employees):

1. Clearly defined expectations. Few things are more motivating, effective or efficient than a competent, trained, experienced employee who knows what is expected ("who, what, when") and is empowered to do what they were hired to do. Conversely, the employee who has little, conflicting or no direction is de-motivated, inefficient and ineffective. Employees often complain of wasted efforts, rework and mistakes caused by inadequate communication of what is expected.

2. Resources to do the job. It's unfair and unreasonable to expect employees to do a proper job without the proper resources. If resources are limited, employees need realistic expectations in alignment with available resources. In tough times, management and employees have to

---

[3] Marcus Buckingham & Curt Coffman, *First, Break All The Rules* ((Simon & Schuster, 1999). The comprehensive, worldwide poll asked participants of many nationalities to rate their level of satisfaction in a number of key areas. The results identified what *the most productive employees* want and/or need from an organization.

identify alternative solutions that don't require additional funding. It's achievable, but breaking through the nay-saying and "I can't" requires on-going, clear communication between management and employees.

3. Opportunity to apply skills and talents. We've found that every organization has a "hidden workforce" with skills, expertise and talents that are unused, undiscovered, or both. Most employees are waiting to be given the opportunity to show what they can do. You can achieve significantly more productivity within your current staffing levels by removing constraints to this untapped resource. The more skilled and experienced the work force, the better equipped they are to help management meet objectives. Unfortunately, this resource is often neglected because organizations lack a management system to effectively tap into it.

4. Regular recognition. Sadly, the majority of people we've met don't feel valued at work. In almost every employee opinion survey we've conducted, recognition is included in the top five areas needing improvement. For the most part, what employees are really asking for is genuine appreciation for their contributions and acknowledgment for their effort and hard work. Interestingly, the majority of managers and supervisors with whom we've worked regretfully acknowledge their weakness in this area. Most express that they think about giving recognition and want to follow through, but that the opportunity to do so gets quickly lost in the demands on their time. We've had many supervisors tell us, "I'm so bad at this; I need help with ideas and something to remind me on a regular basis". Frankly, this is one of the easiest problems to solve.

5. Supervisor who demonstrates caring. An employee's immediate supervisor is the most important person in the organization in terms of impact on the employee's development, contribution and job satisfaction. The supervisor/employee relationship is critical to developing effective communication, cooperation and productivity within a workgroup, division, department, and with customers. Caring equals valuing people in general, and demonstrating it one-on-one. To an employee, genuine caring is demonstrated by the supervisor who deals with the "whole" person; who takes all aspects into consideration. We've had supervisors ask us, "You mean I have to act like I care?" And they were serious.

6. Encouragement to develop. This means a supervisor has to spend time assessing each direct report's skill levels and training needs, in relation to the needs of the organization.

7. Input/opinions valued. We all have opinions and when possible and prudent, want the opportunity to have our input heard and valued. Employees are most engaged, enthusiastic and committed when they are given the opportunity to give input, get feedback on their input, participate in solutions and see the impact of their contributions. Each of these four components is important; employees don't just want the opportunity to give input; they want to know that their input is taken seriously.

8. Organizational mission that inspires and engages employees. We've heard employees refer to management's annual planning retreat as the "hallucination in the woods" time. Clearly there was no respect for the outcome, let alone inspiration. In our experience, most employees want to be inspired by and engaged in a meaningful mission.

A meaningful mission is created by many authors. The original draft may be created in a variety of ways:

- By top management
- By a management team
- By a cross-functional department team

It really doesn't matter how the draft starts. What does matter is how it's developed and refined. Distribute it to employees and ask for feedback. Create 2-3 drafts from the feedback and distribute those. Continue the process until you've refined it to a point of diminishing return.

Make the mission the boss. Every problem, activity, idea, solution should be run through the filter of the mission. Does it support our mission? Will it help us achieve our mission? Is this in conflict with our mission? You don't have to wait for the finished product to do this. Your first draft is good enough to provide a beacon for everyone in the organization. Although your final product will probably look a lot different than the original, the underlying principles will most likely be the same.

9. Accountability for quality work. After years of meeting and working with thousands of employees, we can pretty quickly gauge cooperation and productivity levels in an individual. In 1-on-1 employee interviews, employees typically share one of the following with us:

- They'd like to get regular feedback from their supervisors; they want to know how they can improve, and want to be held accountable. They'd like everyone to be held accountable to the same standards of behavior and performance. Without fail, employees who are cooperative and productive respond in this manner. Not only are they unthreatened by accountability, they seek it. They also want and need management to hold slackers and behavioral misfits accountable. This is fair, reasonable and good business sense, because disruptive behavior and poor individual performance negatively impact group performance.
- They want others (everyone else but them) to be held accountable. Notice the absence of personal accountability? Without fail, employees with behavior and/or performance problems go on the attack and blame everyone but themselves for a group's problems. They claim favoritism, the "good old boy" network and fear of retaliation as root causes of their problems with management. Unfortunately, we know that these symptoms do exist in some organizations; they're a serious detriment to morale and productivity. We also know from experience that most work groups have a small percentage of people (the toxic 5%) who wave these terms around like red flags to avoid personal accountability.

If you want to retain your best employees, it's imperative that fair, objective performance and behavioral standards are defined, communicated and reinforced through modeling and accountability.

10. Friendship/camaraderie. This directly relates to the "belongingness" need. Work is supposed to provide more than an income; it should enhance quality of life. People are at their best in a work environment that is friendly, cordial, professional and supportive. Camaraderie is forged through teamwork; colleagues accomplishing common objectives together. We aren't referring to a shallow, "feel-good" program that best case provides a band-aid solution and worst case disenfranchises employees. Many managers and directors dismiss these programs as "that touchy-feely stuff" that takes people away from getting important "real work" done. We agree with them. In our experience, friendship and camaraderie happen naturally as workgroup members achieve relevant, measurable objectives together through teamwork.

11. Feedback on performance. If we had to list the number one problem that most organizations have in common, it would have to be communication. Lack of communication or poor communication is cited in every interview, opinion survey and focus group that we've ever conducted. Frankly, this employee input is the motivation for our performance management system for feedback. Employees need to know if (and to what degree) they're meeting expectations. For feedback to be meaningful, it needs to be timely and specific.

Even though your best employees motivate themselves and will continue to work hard with or without timely feedback, they deserve it. It's in the organization's best interests to invest time in and attention to these people. Once you've spent a few minutes with a high-performing employee, you can turn them loose, confident that there are no hidden issues; they understand and agree with what's expected and know how to deliver. Time spent in regular communication with your best employees will yield a much greater return than the disproportionate amount of time spent with problem employees.

Timely feedback is especially critical for accountability. Repeatedly, we've had to address employee behavioral and performance problems because their supervisor has failed to give them timely feedback on a number of seemingly "small" issues. When people don't get feedback that there's a problem, they assume everything is okay and continue doing what they're doing. Bottom line, people are allowed to get away with bad behavior and performance. By the time the problem escalates into something larger, it's difficult for the supervisor to hold them accountable because the employee can rightfully say, "This is the first time I've heard that it was a problem."

12. Opportunities to learn/grow. It makes better sense to retain productive, valuable staff than to repeatedly go through the hiring and training process. Talented, motivated people want and need work environments that offer growth and learning opportunities. Creating these opportunities should be a deliberate effort undertaken in partnership between employees and their immediate supervisor. Growth and learning are most effective when incorporated into a development plan that's focused on contributing to department objectives.

In the modern world of knowledge work, creativity, innovation and continuous improvement, the essential virtues needed are in every employee. You nurture those values when you give employees a greater sense of ownership and control over their jobs. You impart the sense of ownership when you actively listen, back them up, demonstrate trust and respect, give them feedback, then leave them alone.

Customer Relations

A company's most vital asset is its customers. Without them, you would not and could not exist in business. When you satisfy your customers, they not only help you grow by continuing to do business with you, but help formulate a positive perception and image in the marketplace.

The first step in achieving customer satisfaction is to listen to their needs. Hearing the "voice of the customer" is critical to capturing the requirements/feedback from the customer (internal or external) in order to provide them with the best service. This process for hearing the customers' needs is all about being proactive and constantly innovating to capture the changing requirements of the customers over time.

The "voice of the customer" is the term used to describe the stated and unstated needs or requirements of the customer. The voice of the customer can be captured in a variety of ways: Direct discussion or interviews, surveys, focus groups, customer specifications, observation, warranty data, field reports, complaint logs, etc. The information collected is used to identify the quality attributes needed for satisfactory service.

Customer feedback data will fall into five categories[4], all of which must be met in order to satisfy your customer.

1. Reliability – keeping the promises made to the customer.
There are three types of promises:

- Personal
- Organizational
- Expected

Establishing realistic promises with the customer helps reduce the possibility of broken ones. Promise less than you can deliver (under-promise, over-deliver). Sometimes it is not possible to keep a promise. When a broken promise occurs:

- Apologize
- Admit something is wrong
- Find out what needs to be done
- Make sure you don't make the same mistake twice
- Use problem-solving tools to find and fix the root cause of the problem

2. Responsiveness – doing things in a timely fashion.
Taking the following actions will help you to actively practice responsiveness:

- Create realistic deadlines
- Ask the customer for their input
- Address delays

---

[4] Performance Research Associates, Inc: Delivering Knock Your Socks off Service (New York: AMACOM, 1991)

3. Assurance – demonstrating competence and confidence.
To provide assurance to the customer, combine substance and style; what you do and how you do it assures the customer that you know and care about the product/service you provide.

Substance:

- Product/service knowledge
- Organizational knowledge
- Interpersonal skills
- Problem-solving skills

Style:

- First impressions
- Communications
- Non-verbal communications

4. Empathy – treating customers as individuals.
Quite often, a problem is not what drives disgruntled customers away; it is the lack of empathy perceived by the customer. Many times customers will be tolerant and understanding of complications and problems that arise. What they will not tolerate is callous indifference to their plight.
It is important at this point to differentiate between empathy and sympathy.

5. Tangibles – visible proof of the quality of service provided.
Service is such an intangible commodity that it is often difficult for the customer to realize its presence, much less its worth. It is essential that you, as the service provider, convey the value of the service transaction's intangible aspects through a physical demonstration.

- Take pride in both your appearance and that of the materials you give to your customer
- When customers give their name and telephone number, write it down and read it back to them; this demonstrates that they are important to you and the organization, and offers assurance that it is your intention to get back to them

- Ensure the workplace areas your customers see are clean, safe, comfortable and as orderly as you can make them

Work Processes and Capabilities

Even in the most structured organizations, many workplace processes are disorganized. Different people carry out processes in different ways or duplicate effort, or the same employee does something different each time. Documentation may be incomplete or outdated. This is stressful for employees and costly for organizations.

Most processes don't start out this way, but over time, small changes occur and different procedures develop. Work gets done and no one gives it any strategic thought or considers how it may affect overall performance. People adapt their thinking to compensate for inefficiency and make it work.

This is an opportunity for process improvement using lean principles. The lean philosophy emphasizes creating more value for customers through waste reduction and workflow optimization. The outcome is a more organized operation where employees have ready access to the tools they need, they are empowered to deliver outstanding customer service, and costs are reduced due to more efficient processes. The improvements in work processing lead to better bottom line performance.

While implementing lean process improvements can be complicated, the basic principles are not. For most organizations, lean management can be carried out rather simply in the following steps.

1. Focus service on adding value to your customers. Value creation occurs when the quality of services received is perceived as high compared to their cost. Using "voice of the customer" surveys, determine what your customers value the most and how to provide it better, faster and at lower production cost.

2. Assess how work gets done. Often, assumptions are made about how work gets done without knowing what actually does happen. During day-to-day operations we don't often think about how work gets done and often do it poorly. To maximize value and reduce wasteful activities, processes and procedures need to be analyzed for improvement opportunities.

3. Eliminate waste. Once you've assessed the process and work procedures for improvement potential, look at steps in the process that don't directly create value for the customer. Refine and improve your process flow to eliminate non-valued-added activity such as wasted time, wasted movement, wasted inventory, customer delays, waiting for approvals, delays, unnecessary steps, duplication of effort, errors and rework. Collect data and manage improved processes with facts. Confirm changes are working. Continue to eliminate errors and waste to continuously improve value to customers.

4. Empower the people doing the work. The best person to improve a process is the one working on it day after day. Use employees' experience and expertise to help identify new processing methods.

5. Standardize process and work procedures. Without control mechanisms in place, processes naturally decay and begin generating waste. Formally document your procedures to capture all improvements and ensure consistent output. Make sure everyone doing the work follows standard operating procedure. Replicating process improvements consistently is the key to delivering sustained value to customers.

Strategy

Strategic plans all tend to look pretty much the same[5]. They usually have three major parts. The first is a vision or mission statement that sets out a relatively lofty and inspirational or "noble" goal. The second is a list of goals and initiatives that the organization will carry out in pursuit of the vision and mission. A third element is the conversion of the initiatives into business unit action plans with detailed activities defined for one year. Management typically commits to only one year in the context of a three to five year plan.

---

[5] The Big Lie of Strategic Planning, Harvard Business Review, January – February 2014

While strategic plans are one of the most widely used "best management practices" and they are important to an organization's success, you're bound to encounter challenges with implementation. Here are 10 reasons why they fail[6]. Our approach to Strategic Planning will help you avoid these traps.

1. Having a plan simply for plan's sake. Some organizations go through the motions of developing a plan simply because every good organization must have a plan. Often this approach creates a document but does nothing to increase the organization's ability to respond to change. And it does nothing to help people synchronize the many moving parts of the organization. You get out of a plan what you put into it. You must do it right and use it right.

2. Not focusing on results. Management must pay attention to changes in the business environment, set meaningful priorities, understand the need to target the critical business issues and pursue the right results.

3. Limited commitment. Senior executives must be fully committed and fully understand how a strategic plan can improve their organization. "Maverick" and "cowboy" activities outside the plan cannot and must not be tolerated. The Plan is followed, or it gets formally changed as needed, and management recommits to the revised Plan.

4. Not having the right people involved. Those charged with executing the plan should be involved from the onset. If the right people are involved in creating the plan they will be committed to seeing it through to execution.

5. Not using the plan as a guide. This is as bad as not writing a plan at all. If a plan is to be an effective management tool, it must be followed and reviewed continually. Strategic plans decay rapidly if not continually used and reviewed.

---

[6] 10 Reasons Strategic Plans Fail, Forbes, 11/30/2011

6. Unwillingness or inability to change. Your organization and your strategic plan must be dynamic and able to adapt as market conditions change. Make your plan a "working document" that is flexible and comprehends the changing external environment.

7. Having the wrong people in leadership positions. Management must be willing to make the tough decisions to ensure the right individuals are in the right leadership positions. The "right" individuals include those who will advocate for and champion the strategic plan and help keep the organization on track.

8. Ignoring marketplace reality, facts, and assumptions. When it comes to marketplace realities, don't discount potential problems because they have not made an immediate impact on your organization. Plan in advance to be ready for external changes when they do occur.

9. No accountability or follow through. Be tough once the plan is developed and resources are committed. Ensure there are consequences for not delivering on the strategy.

10. Unrealistic goals or lack of focus and resources. Strategic plans must be focused and include a manageable number of goals, objectives, and programs. Be sure there are adequate resources to accomplish all goals and objectives.

By avoiding these pitfalls, you can create an effective planning process, create a realistic direction for the future, and greatly improve the chances for successful implementation of your strategy.

Linking, Aligning and Balancing the Four Key Competencies

To be successful with the model, all four components must be simultaneously addressed in the planning and execution steps of the organizational development process. The framework can be as simple or as comprehensive as you choose. To start, these should be some of the questions you answer for each competency:

1. Employee and Work Culture. What elements in our organization most contribute to the company's ability to innovate, improve, and learn? Do we measure employee satisfaction?

2. Customer Relations. Who is our customer? How do our customers perceive our company? How can we best understand the loyalty of our customers across the various touch points in our organization? What outcomes do they value most? How is customer value driving our attention and resources?

3. Work Processes. What must our company excel at? How successful is the execution of our company's key business processes? What metrics best indicate both efficient and effective performance?

4. Strategy. What are our strategic boundaries? What are our most urgent and critical performance variables? Have we established specific, measurable goals? Is strategy clearly communicated to employees?

We strongly suggest starting with a simple framework and developing it over time. After measuring customer satisfaction, employee satisfaction, financials and process productivity, you can make adjustments for improvement. Additional elements can be added and refined by evaluating the "best practices" that are working in other organizations.

CHAPTER 4

Process for Organizational Development

An Intuitive Process

Having gone through the organizational development process with thousands of people, we've gotten the impression that the methods we use are intuitive for most people. Our process is the same as what people use to manage their lives on a daily basis. Whether cleaning the garage, planning a vacation, or cooking a meal, we tend to intuitively process actions today so we realize benefits in the future. Our process is that simple.

Based on our needs for a specific outcome, we tend to naturally go through a series of steps to work efficiently toward a result that satisfies the need. The typical progression of steps includes:

1. Assess what's needed and why
2. Plan for time, resources, and any obstacles
3. Align all resources needed for the expected outcome
4. Learn new information required to get the planned result
5. Take synchronized action
6. Measure success or failure
7. Review for results and lessons learned

The 7-Step Process

The *7-Step Process™* described in the following pages is a proprietary methodology developed by Childress Consulting to effectively generate positive organizational change in a timely manner. The process creates an organizational system that is focused on job performance from top to bottom. Throughout the process, employees are treated as valued partners in planning, implementing, measuring and reviewing progress. Openness defines the relationship between management and employees. This relationship carries over into customer relations. As with any tool, the *7-Step Process™* should be **adapted** to address the **specific needs and culture** of each department/organization. It should be customized so that it will successfully drive problem-solving and improvement efforts. The goal of implementing this process should be to create and sustain a cooperative, problem-solving environment focused on providing value-added services to internal and external customers.

Why use this process?

The seven steps will quickly and simultaneously achieve business performance improvement and competency in four key competency areas: Customer Satisfaction, Employee Development and Satisfaction, Work Process Efficiency, and Business Strategy.

What characterizes this process?

Over a short period of time, a spirit of cooperation develops. Once employees learn that they can trust this new development, they become eager and energetic about problem-solving. As each element of the process is undertaken, new learning unfolds, helping to determine what specific steps will be taken next. Although "mechanical" in that it has a specific set of elements, the process is in reality "dynamic," responding to the specific needs and circumstances of each organization. As such, it should be customized for each organization.

What are the expected outcomes of the process?

Outcomes for individual employees include: continuous improvement in behavior, job performance and job satisfaction.

Outcomes for the organization include: continuous improvement in productivity, quality of work, customer relations, financial performance and morale.

What is expected of each person throughout this process?

Employees are expected to show commitment to and demonstration of continuous personal improvement in behavior and performance, and contribute to team efforts. A "Performance Management Process" defines and manages the success plan for the organization and its employees. The intent of a performance management process is to encourage employees to take responsibility for ensuring their own job security. Working with their supervisor, the employee defines a plan that helps them reach their full potential in the current job. Regular feedback, positive and constructive, is critical to a successful performance management system. Rather than wait until the annual appraisal review, the supervisor and employee will periodically review the employee's progress against expectations and goals. Interim coaching is done both formally and informally. Interim coaching should be done at least twice/year in addition to the employee's annual evaluation.

The 7 Steps to Success in Organizational Development

1. Assessment. Purpose: Key in on critical business issues and opportunities for improvement.

In the *7-Step Process™*, informal and/or formal assessment is on-going to measure progress and improvement and to identify problem-solving/improvement opportunities.

Tools for assessing and evaluating organizational performance may include:

- Employee/customer opinion surveys
- Focus groups
- Management reviews
- Team self-assessments

- "Skip-Level" meetings
- 1-on-1 interviews
- Statistical data collection and analysis
- Performance measures

2. **Planning.** Purpose: Develop a strategic plan with goals/objectives that address feedback gleaned from your assessments. Departments will define strategies that support and help accomplish corporate strategic goals.

A series of "Search and Planning Sessions" are needed to develop the framework and detail of an organizational and/or department strategic plan. Your plan should include:

- **Vision**—developed by the lead management person in the organization or department for which the strategic plan is being developed. (If the plan is for a department, it would be the department director. The department director's vision should support the overall organizational vision.)
- **Mission**—developed with feedback from all members of the organization for which it is being written.
- **Values**—developed with input from everyone. Usually comprised of 7-10 key values with a brief clarifying definition.
- **Code of Conduct**—developed with input from everyone, this is a list of behavioral expectations of all employees in the organization—defines the standard of behavior by which the organization/department will operate.
- **Goals/Objectives**—developed by brainstorming, using the feedback from assessments. Most common goals include: Customer Service and Satisfaction, Employee Development and Satisfaction, Internal Process Improvements, and Financial Performance Improvements. Objectives are identified for each. Goals should be broad; examples would be: improve profit, improve customer satisfaction. Objectives for each goal should be "SMART": Specific, Measurable, Achievable, Results-oriented and Time-bound. Each manager must have at least one "stretch objective" in their Performance Plan

- **Action Plan**—developed to focus activities on goals and objectives. Specific actions (what) are defined with responsibilities (who) and due dates (when) for accountability.

3. Alignment. Purpose: Ensure common goals and everyone on the same page.

Everyone and everything in the department/organization aligns with the strategic plan. That includes management, employees and processes. Alignment for departments is ensured through regular "Plan, Do, Review" sessions. Individual employees achieve alignment through the Performance Management Process. Coaching of individuals and teams is necessary during this step.

4. Training/People Development. Purpose: Develop skill set required to accomplish Strategic Plan.

Training needs identified in assessments are incorporated into goals/objectives in Employee Development. Training will usually focus on three key competencies:

- Technical—specific job-related skills, process and problem-solving tools.
- Administrative—management, team and process-related.
- Emotional (interpersonal and intrapersonal)—communication skills, awareness and management of emotions and stress.

Technical and administrative competencies focus on performance; emotional competencies focus on behavior.

5. Implementation. Purpose: Convert Strategic Plan to action.

"Who, what, when" actions are defined for strategic plan objectives. Breaking goals/objectives into incremental pieces with a timeline distributes the work of achieving the strategic plan across the board. Timelines hold people accountable to doing what they say they'll do. Tracking actions on a "Project Plan Sheet" is most efficient and effective for planning, implementation and review. Scheduling formal review sessions drives completion of actions.

6. Measurement. Purpose: Keep score of success or failure

Management and teams agree on defined measures to determine progress/success. Typical measurements include customer satisfaction, cycle time, labor reduction, cost reduction, employee satisfaction, employee safety, employee productivity, attendance, elimination of waste, reduction in defects, increase in revenue/profit, streamlined processes. There should be measurable improvement in productivity, quality of work, customer service and employee morale. (Commitment to this process typically results in a 30% increase in productivity, i.e. value-added output per employee).

7. Review. Purpose: Accountability and refinement.

The *7-Step Process*™ is iterative. Review is a crucial step for accountability, reinforcement and renewal. It is on-going; formally and informally. Regularly scheduled reviews hold people accountable to both results and alignment to the process and strategic plan. In the remaining chapters, the *7-Step Process*™ is shown in a straight-forward methodology designed to create a customized management system for the user.

CHAPTER 5

Road Map for Organizational Development

Create an Annual Plan

In this chapter we provide a typical process, and timeline, to get OD underway and driving cultural change. The process is also shown in the flow chart at the end of this chapter.

For employees to take the new work routines seriously, senior management must actively engage in leading the effort to drive the organizational development process forward. The senior executive must be seen as the primary champion responsible for directing organizational development; it cannot be relegated to subordinates. He/She must insist on accountability for measurable outcomes. If the process and methods are followed, management can expect measurable progress on strategic goals within a few months.

Activities for the First 90 Days

1. Begin Leadership Development
2. Communicate Plan to employees (schedule all hands meetings, memos, etc.)
3. Complete Assessments (survey internal and external stakeholders)
4. Complete Strategic Plan (create alignment across the organization)
    a. Master Plan
    b. Departmental Plans
    c. Employee Performance Plans
    d. Organization Work Culture and Change Management Plan

5. Establish a communication plan and an ongoing process for accountability
6. Execute Plans (take action defined in plan)
7. Schedule first Accountability Review (measurable results should be seen in the first 90 days or less)
    a. What were the goals/objectives?
    b. What actions were taken?
    c. What are the results after 90 days>
8. Plan next 90 Day Cycle

Quarterly Cycle (complete this "Plan, Deploy, Review" process every 90 days)

1. Managers Plan/Align/Realign/Synchronize their efforts after each 90 day review
2. Assess progress and any disconnects
    a. Leadership Team
    b. Department Managers with their Work Groups
3. Take action (re-alignment across the organization is leadership driven)
    a. Update and refine Operational Work Plans
    b. Cascade down to working level via employee Performance Plans
    4. Review/Accountability (aimed at meeting strategic objectives driven by leadership
    a. Repeat the "Plan, Deploy, Review" cycle every 90 days
    b. KPIs and Performance Measures show progress

End of 12 months

1. Formal Review (accountability organization-wide)
2. Complete new assessment of progress, disconnects, lessons learned
3. Improvements needed (prioritized and categorized as major or minor)
4. Define general direction alignment across the organization
5. Strategic Planning workshop

Complete no later than 13 months

1. Complete new Strategic Plan document for the upcoming year
2. Distribute Strategic Plan to all employees
3. Complete Departmental Plans
4. Complete Employee Performance Plans
5. Initiate deployment of new Strategic Plan

How the Culture will Change

Be aware that it takes three to four 90-day performance cycles (9-12 months) for managers and employees to gain a comfort level with the performance culture. Some people will be comfortable very early in the process, others require more time to adjust, and some will struggle. At any rate, by the end of one year, everyone is expected to be on board, aligned, action-oriented, and accountable.

Also be aware that to create a culture of execution, people must have a desire to follow something worthwhile. In order for them to line up with management they must be kept apprised of management's direction. They need to know why the particular strategy is relevant; it needs to make sense. They need to have help with developing their abilities related to new processes and expectations. And, most importantly, management must reinforce the significance of the cultural change by being consistent with their message, actions and expectations.

Organizational Development Flow Chart

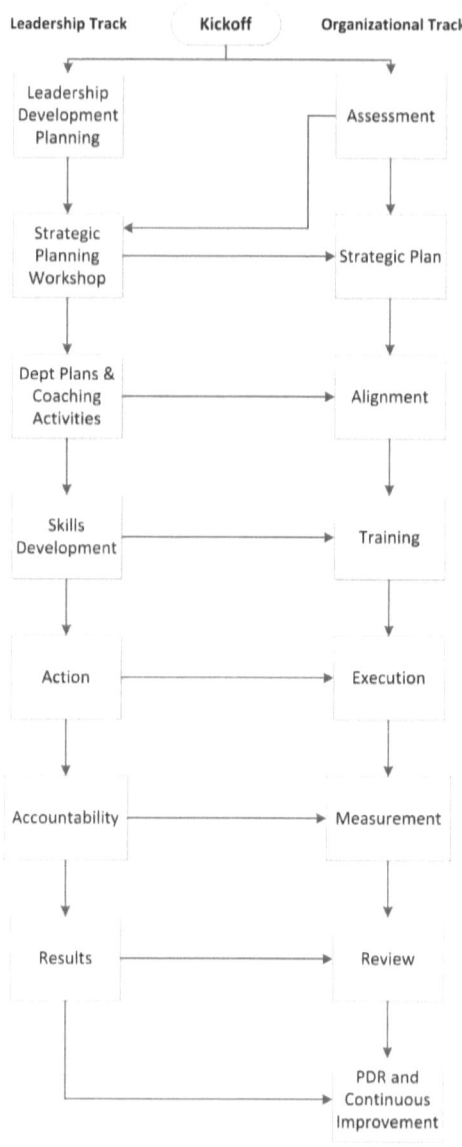

CHAPTER 6

Tool Kit for Organizational Development

This chapter lists the tools and resources we commonly use. There are many useful and effective tools for OD implementation and each organization should determine the ones most useful to them.

In our process, the Tool Kit elements are used as needed to support the OD Plan. Tools must be ready when needed to allow the OD process to work and progress forward. Tool Kit creation and use must be specified as objectives in your Strategic Plan.

First Tool: 90 Day Checklist for Managers

Prior to any major OD activity taking place, create a detailed list of objectives and action items you plan to complete in the first 90 days. The 90 day checklist will include some, if not all, of the following:

1. Communication Plan
2. Kickoff Activities
3. Assessments
4. Leadership Training
5. Strategic Plan
6. Departmental Plans
7. Employee Performance Plans
8. Training Plan
9. Change Management and Work Culture Plan
10. First Accountability Review

Tools for Assessments

1. Employee/customer opinion surveys
2. Focus groups
3. Management reviews
4. Team self-assessments
5. "Skip-Level" meetings
6. 1-on-1 interviews
7. Data Collection, Analysis and Reporting

Tools for Leadership Training and Development

1. 360 degree evaluations
2. Leadership development action plans
3. Leadership training needs assessment
4. Organizational development workshops
    a. Workshop curriculum and course outline
    b. Workshop expectations, goals, agenda, etc.
    c. Workshop Facilitator's Guide
    d. Participant's Guide
    e. Checklist for practical application of new learning
5. Accountability reviews
    a. Agenda
    b. Objectives
    c. Progress Reports
    d. Next Steps

Tools for Supervisor Training (Boot Camp)

1. Curriculum and course outlines
2. Expectations, goals, agenda, outcomes, etc.
3. Facilitator's Guide for trainer
4. Participant's Guides for Learning Modules
    a. Expectations and Responsibilities of Supervisors
    b. Interpersonal Skills and Team Dynamics
    c. Employee Development

d. Customer Service
e. Managing Workload of Self and Staff
f. Problem-Solving
g. Work Process Improvement
h. Budget and other Financial Management
5. Self-directed learning plan (develop job skills, coaching from manager)
6. Checklist for practical application of new learning
7. Accountability Reviews with manager

Tools for Employee Training and Development

1. Training Needs Assessment
2. Curriculum and course outlines
   a. Interpersonal Skills
   b. Technical Skills
   c. Administrative Skills
3. Training Delivery Tools
   a. Classroom
   b. Online
   c. Coaching
   d. On the job training

Tools and Resources for Work Culture Development

1. Senior management assigns members to a cross-functional "Work Culture Team"
2. Cross-functional team is chartered to identify issues, solutions, and take action)
   a. The Team follows a prescribed process for change management
   b. Goals for culture are performance and behavior based
   c. The Team makes recommendations to management to address growth and advancement opportunities
   d. The Team works to define the best culture and its features
   e. Team uses "Results-Oriented Meetings" process
3. Team gives formal report at Quarterly Review

Tools for Employee Performance Management

1. Performance Plans
2. Coaching Plans
3. Improvement Plans

Tools and Guidelines for Meetings

1. Daily standup "Production Meetings" to distribute workload and prioritize activities
2. Weekly "Staff Meetings" to manage the "Plan, Do, Review" cycle
3. Monthly Review (Minor Performance Cycle, department focused)
   a. Goals and objectives from last month and how they help drive the strategy
   b. Accomplishments
   c. Obstacles, Challenges
   d. Include discussion of the external environment
   e. Next Steps
   f. Evaluate Meeting effectiveness
4. Quarterly Review/Planning (Major Performance Cycle, organization focused)
5. Annual Strategy Session (Major Planning Cycle)

Tools for Process Improvements

1. Benchmarking for structure, procedures, improvement and measurements
2. Process mapping and streamlining (lean principles)
3. Standardized work procedures
4. Mistake-proofing and quality assurance
5. Problem-solving
6. Continuous improvement

In Summary

When the key elements of employees, customers, purposeful work, and a strategic vision come together effectively, people are energized. Energized people begin to share a common vision and different levels and functions realize the enormous potential that resides in them and their co-workers. If this energy is consistently directed at a worthwhile purpose, and not wasted on trivial activities, a performance culture will unfold dynamically. This positive creative energy is fragile and easily destroyed. People will retreat if their needs for reinforcement aren't met. Therefore, management must be vigilant with words and actions that boost the energy, and careful to not destroy it.

We have seen this development process achieve unbelievable results in some of our most difficult organizational development and turnaround projects. We've seen individuals go from toxic to superstar status in just a few months once they realize the positive energy is real and lasting. It truly is a transformational progression.

If cultivated, protected and reinforced, the "culture" becomes the natural environment where people and institutions realize their potential and feel the exhilaration of winning.

About the Author

Quin Childress is the principal of Childress Consulting, a management and human resource consulting firm.

Prior to consulting with private and public sector agencies, Quin served as engineering manager, manufacturing manager, and director of operations for a number of companies in the microelectronics manufacturing industry, including National Semiconductor and Olin Corporation. At Olin, he managed a diverse workforce of 800 employees representing more than 20 different ethnic cultures. As a consultant he has led turnaround and organizational development assignments in large and small businesses as well as federal, state, county and local governments.